GOD'S PURPOSE FOR THE WAIT

Restarting Life With God After A Breakup

GOD'S PURPOSE
FOR THE WAIT

Restarting Life With God After A Breakup

VICKI L. OLTON

PUBLISHING

BARBADOS

GOD'S PURPOSE FOR THE WAIT: Restarting Life With God After A Breakup

All Scripture quotations are taken from the *King James Version* unless otherwise indicated.

Scripture quotations marked MSG are taken from *The Message Bible*

Scripture quotations marked HCSB are taken from the *Holman Christian Standard Bible*

Paperback ISBN: 978-1974051229

Published by Divine Purpose Publishing in Barbados

Printed in the United States of America

For more information on this book and related materials, visit www.vickiolton.com.

When We Seek God First, He Will Gives Us What We Need According to His Will

"Has anyone by fussing in front of the mirror ever gotten taller by so much as an inch? All this time and money wasted on fashion—do you think it makes that much difference? Instead of looking at the fashions, walk out into the fields and look at the wildflowers. They never primp or shop, but have you ever seen color and design quite like it? The ten best-dressed men and women in the country look shabby alongside them.

"If God gives such attention to the appearance of wildflowers—most of which are never even seen—don't you think he'll attend to you, take pride in you, do his best for you? What I'm trying to do here is to get you to relax, to not be so preoccupied with getting, so you can respond to God's giving. People who don't know God and the way he works fuss over these things, but you know both God and how he works. Steep your life in God-reality, God-initiative, God-provisions. Don't worry about missing out. You'll find all your everyday human concerns will be met.

"Give your entire attention to what God is doing right now, and don't get worked up about what may or may not happen tomorrow. God will help you deal with whatever hard things come up when the time comes.

(Matthew 6:27-34 – MSG)

WAIT ON GOD

Wait on the Lord: be of good courage,
and he shall strengthen thine heart: wait, I
say, on the Lord. (Psalm 27:14 - KJV)

Our soul waiteth for the Lord: he is our help
and our shield. (Psalm 33:20 - KJV)

Rest in the Lord, and wait patiently for him:
fret not thyself because of him who
prospereth in his way, because of the man
who bringeth wicked devices to pass.
(Psalm 37:7 - KJV)

Wait on the Lord, and keep his way, and
he shall exalt thee to inherit the land: when
the wicked are cut off, thou shalt see it.
(Psalm 37:34 - KJV)

Thou wilt keep him in perfect peace,
whose mind is stayed on thee: because he
trusteth in thee. (Isaiah 26:3 - KJV)

But they that wait upon the Lord shall
renew their strength; they shall mount up
with wings as eagles; they shall run, and
not be weary; and they shall walk, and not
faint. (Isaiah 40:31 - KJV)

Table of Contents

Dedication

I dedicate this book to the Almighty God.

To all singles; non-Christians and Christians, who have experienced a relationship breakup and need a new start with God.

Lastly, I dedicate this book to all who desire to understand the importance of God's waiting process.

Foreword

If you have experienced a relationship breakup, a new start is just what you need!

This new start will not be like any other you have ever experienced because you are going to restart your life with God, this time around.

God's Purpose For The Wait teaches that restarting life with God means that you are making a decision to wait on God. When you wait on God, you give Him permission to take total control in every area of your life.

This is your time of change!

God does not want you to run to another partner for comfort. He wants you to run into His arms.

There is a process of spiritual, emotional, mental and physical healing that God wants to take **YOU** through. As He does this, He will not only prepare you for the blessing of marriage in His perfect timing but most importantly, He will prepare you to walk in the divine purpose for which you were created.

Preface

I knew God was calling me to let go of a relationship and surrender my all to Him. As much as it hurt, I had to be obedient to God's direction.

This was not the time for me to run to another man, but since God led me into the wait, it was the time to allow Him to heal me, especially from the emotional pain of separation.

My original thought was that **God's purpose for the wait** was to primarily prepare me for marriage. But I was wrong. God simply wanted me to focus on being healed and most importantly He wanted to reveal the powerful purpose for which He placed me on this earth.

During my waiting process God started to reveal that He calls us into a waiting season for a number of reasons. The wait is actually God's process of healing, deliverance, restoration and preparation for purpose.

The more I waited, the more God showed me the hindrances and blockages that existed in my life that had led me to make bad decisions in the past, even in past relationships. God knows all and sees all. I shudder to think of the mess that I could have continued in, had I not given up on what was not working. Had I not let go, and held on to my God, even His will for me to write this book would have been hindered.

God wants you to know that the wait is like His checkpoint where He reveals to us everything that is hindering us from going forward in the plan that He created for us. At the checkpoint, He reveals what is not for us and how He wants us to live for Him. He shows us the deep and hidden things that we cannot see that have held us back all this time from living the life He had planned for us from the beginning. If we do not enter this checkpoint we could end up in serious problems, moving from relationship to relationship. The devil's plan is to keep us form reaching this checkpoint by enticing us to run to another partner after a breakup.

This book is therefore based on my experience of waiting on God after a relationship breakup and the things which God taught me and brought me through during the wait.

God wanted me to share this experience as an example and guide to those who may think that restarting with another partner is the best thing to do.

God wants you to restart your life with Him this time around because He has much to change in you and to reveal to you. By refusing to restart with God you can continue running into a cycle of breakups and remain out of God's perfect will. Do you want this for your life?

As you read, may you see past all desires for another partner. May you allow God to clean up all the dirt of your past so that your beautiful future of purpose can be unveiled.

At the end of this book are special prayers for the single woman and man. A short journal is also included, in which you may record any revelations and thoughts.

Introduction

Relationship breakups sometimes result in emotional, mental, spiritual and even physical pain.

There is no person who can provide the deep comfort, love and spiritual healing that you need after a breakup. Only God can!

So today God is telling you to restart your life with Him and not with another man or woman. Stop seeking a partner to make you feel good. Wait on God!

The Bible states that God is a healer, so it is safe to turn to Him:

He healeth the broken in heart, and bindeth up their wounds. (Psalm 147:3 - KJV)

Even if there was no pain involved in your breakup, and you have made a decision that it is time to move on, God wants you to move on with Him.

Why?

God wants you to become a true worshipper according to His original plan. He wants to become the center of your life. His desire is for you to depend on Him and of course, He wants to make sure that you do not move on in any kind of broken state.

God Wants You to:

… seek ye first the kingdom of God, and his righteousness; and all these things shall be added unto you. (Matthew 6:33 - KJV)

I want you to be without concerns. An unmarried man is concerned about the things of the Lord—how he may please the Lord. But a married man is concerned about the things of the world—how he may please his wife — and his interests are divided. An unmarried woman or a virgin is concerned about the things of the Lord, so that she may be holy both in body and in spirit. But a married woman is concerned about the things of the world—how she may please her husband (1 Corinthians 7:32-34 – HCSB)

Chapter One

SURELY "THERE ARE MORE FISH IN THE SEA" TO CHOOSE FROM

Be sober, be vigilant; because your adversary the devil, as a roaring lion, walketh about, seeking whom he may devour: (1 Peter 5:8 – KJV)

GOD'S PURPOSE FOR THE WAIT

Why bother about a relationship breakup? As they say, *"there are more fish in the sea"* to choose from.

Although it is true that there are so many others, should this be our mindset? Should we give ourselves the permission to "choose" another man or woman? Should we gamble with our lives like this?

It is wonderful to keep in mind that life goes on after a breakup, but should we pacify our pain with another *"fish"*?

My answer to all these questions is a big **NO**!

The Real Impact of "There Are More Fish In The Sea"

"There are more fish in the sea" is a phrase of comfort. Its purpose is to encourage the hurting person to dismiss the pain and move on with someone else.

First of all, to catch a fish, you need bait. Thus the statement promotes **you**, the woman or man, as **bait**; a piece of meat thrown out for the catch.

When we make a decision to allow this statement to influence our actions, we open the door to the enemy.

GOD'S PURPOSE FOR THE WAIT

Remember that Proverbs 18:21 says:

Death and life are in the power of the tongue: and they that love it shall eat the fruit thereof. (KJV)

So, if you speak about a man or woman as a piece of bait, he or she, unknowing will start to behave like bait. And if you embrace this statement, you will become like the statement.

Understand that bait gets loosely thrown into the water and before you know, you can find yourself loosely going from person to person seeking to be accepted and fulfilled.

God wants you to know that this is a dangerous statement. It grants permission to gamble with our bodies, spirits and souls and can also introduce promiscuity into our lives.

This may be an accepted standard of the world, but it is definitely not God's accepted standard.

GOD'S PURPOSE FOR THE WAIT

Chapter Two

RESTART WITH GOD'S STANDARD

And be not conformed to this world: but be ye transformed by the renewing of your mind, that ye may prove what is that good, and acceptable, and perfect, will of God. (Romans 12:2 – KJV)

Let us restart life today with standard of God!

When we restart with God's standard after a relationship breakup, we make the decision to allow Him to mold our lives by His standard. The standard of the world leads to destruction, but God's standard leads to life.

This is seen in Proverbs 14:12

There is a way that seems right to a man, but its end is the way to death. (HCSB)

Television sitcoms and talk shows promote that happiness comes from the opposite sex. Can I inform you that real happiness and joy comes from God?

Scripture says:

Thou wilt shew me the path of life: in thy presence is fullness of joy; at thy right hand there are pleasures for evermore. (Psalm 16:11 - KJV)

God is calling you to restart your life with Him today by dropping the old standard of the world.

The old standard says that sex before marriage is fine. It gives a broad spectrum of possibilities and tells us that you can live with someone first in order to determine if they are marriage material.

God's standard on the other hand, tells us that we are called to a life of purity in Jesus Christ.

GOD'S PURPOSE FOR THE WAIT

Scripture tells us:

But as the One who called you is holy, you also are to be holy in all your conduct; for it is written, Be holy, because I am holy (1 Peter 1:15 – HCSB)

This is a season in which God wants to change your mindset about relationships and your life in general. God has a preferred standard outlined in the Word of God.

James 4:7 therefore says that you must:

Submit yourselves therefore to God. Resist the devil, and he will flee from you. (KJV)

Are you ready to restart your life with God's standard? If so, hurry on to the next chapter. You will not regret it.

Chapter Three

GOD CALLS US TO REPENT AND BE SAVED

Repent ye therefore, and be converted, that your sins may be blotted out, when the times of refreshing shall come from the presence of the Lord. (Acts 3:19 – KJV)

GOD'S PURPOSE FOR THE WAIT

Restarting life with God after a breakup will be great, but first you have to restart with a clean slate. This means that you need to repent of all the things, which you did according to the world's standard in the past.

There are some errors you have made and some situations you have placed yourself in and you need to tell God that you are sorry. After you repent He wants you to accept Jesus as your Lord and Savior.

Even if you are a Christian, there may be some unrepentant issues, which still remain in your life. You must deal with these things urgently.

Maybe you were in relationships that were not of God. If so, God wants you to repent.

If you have had the *"there are more fish in the sea"* mentality in the past, now is the time to ask God to forgive you. If you have allowed these words to come out of your mouth, God also wants you to repent.

Why?

Matthew12: 36 says:

But I say unto you, That every idle word that men shall speak, they shall give account thereof in the day of judgment. (KJV)

The good thing is that Jesus came and died so that we might be saved:

For when we were yet without strength, in due time Christ died for the ungodly.

For scarcely for a righteous man will one die: yet peradventure for a good man some would even dare to die.
But God commendeth his love toward us, in that, while we were yet sinners, Christ died for us. (Romans 5:6-8 – KJV)

If you are, or were living a life where relationships were the no. 1 priority, you lived a life of idolatry and according to the Scriptures; all idolaters will go to hell.

Know ye not that the unrighteous shall not inherit the kingdom of God? Be not deceived: neither fornicators, nor idolaters, nor adulterers, nor effeminate, nor abusers of themselves with mankind, (1 Corinthians 6:9 – KJV)

Hell is real! Today, God needs you to repent.

14

Some of us have spent so many years putting our trust in man or woman that we became dependent upon them. Over time we lost sight of ourselves; we lost the real understanding of who we really are. We spent so much time trying to be who the other person wanted, rather than being who our God made us to be. Does this sound familiar?

Some of us have fornicated, and prostituted ourselves. Others have disobeyed God and married persons who they knew they should not have married. Lustful desires for sex took over and you did it even though you knew that it was not right.

If any of these scenarios represent you, now is the time to repent and turn your life over to God. Tell God that you are sorry for all your sins and vow today to live a life that is upright in His sight.

If we say that we have no sin, we deceive ourselves, and the truth is not in us.
If we confess our sins, he is faithful and just to forgive us our sins, and to cleanse us from all unrighteousness.
If we say that we have not sinned, we make him a liar, and his word is not in us. (1 John 1:8-10 – KJV)

2 Peter 3:9 goes on to say:

The Lord is not slack concerning his promise, as some men count slackness; but is longsuffering to us-ward, not willing that any should perish, but that all should come to repentance. (KJV)

16

To help you with repentance, you may recite the sinner's prayer:

THE SINNER'S PRAYER

Father in the name of Jesus I acknowledge that I am a sinner and that You are Lord and Savior. I recognize that I need You in my life because You are the giver of life. You can give me a new life and a new start today. Cleanse me of any unbelief. Come into my heart and take control of every area of my life.

I repent for all the sins that I have committed and all the wrongs that I have done in thought, word and deed. Today is the day that I make the decision to walk away from the life that You do not want for me and walk into a new life with You.

Father, I need Your help in every area of my life because I recognize that without You I am nothing nor can I do or be anything without You. Father, I thank You for accepting me into Your kingdom, in the Mighty Name of Jesus, **AMEN!**

Now that you have repented and turned to Jesus Christ, you are considered a new creature in Him according to this Scripture:

Therefore if any man be in Christ, he is a new creature: old things are passed away; behold, all things are become new. (2 Corinthians 5:17 - KJV).

Chapter Four

NOW IT IS TIME TO WAIT

Our soul waiteth for the Lord: he is our help and our shield. (Psalm 33:20 – KJV)

Now that you have cleared up some unfinished business with God, there is one word He wants to tell you:

WAIT!

Don't you dare run to another man or a woman at this stage! I did it over and over and it ran me into trouble. **NOW IT IS TIME TO WAIT!**

You can no longer go back to what you use to be and what you use to do because you have repented. Now you are going forward and restarting your life with God.

You may ask, "Why am I really waiting?"

You are waiting because:

- You do not want to live by the standards of the world anymore, which is sin,
- You want a new start with Jesus,
- You want God to heal you and deliver you from any hindrances from the past that prevented you from being who He called you to be,
- You want your mindset to be like that of Christ and
- You want to embrace God's pure plan for your life and relationships.

There is no doubt that waiting on God produces great benefits because Psalm 27: 14 tells us this:

***Wait** on the LORD: be of good courage, and he shall strengthen thine heart: **wait**, I say, on the LORD (KJV)*.

GOD'S PURPOSE FOR THE WAIT

The Definition Of The Word "Wait"

Dictionary.com defines the word *"wait"* as follows:

"To remain inactive or in a state of repose, as until something expected happens, to remain neglected for a time: to postpone or delay something: to look forward to eagerly".

God is calling you in this season to remain inactive. When you wait there are some things that you have to give up.

Now is the time to put off the sex outside of marriage and seeking another fish in the sea. Now is the time to eagerly expect God to transform your life, not only for marriage, but also for His perfect will. **IT IS TIIME TO WAIT ON GOD!**

Chapter Five

GOD'S PURPOSE FOR THE WAIT

But they that wait upon the Lord shall renew their strength; they shall mount up with wings as eagles; they shall run, and not be weary; and they shall walk, and not faint.
(Isaiah 40:31 - KJV)

GOD'S PURPOSE FOR THE WAIT

God's ultimate goal for the wait is to create men and women of God who will not put the desire for relationships or marriage before a relationship with God.

What Happens When We Wait On God?

When we wait on God, we allow Him to be in the driver seat of our lives. In this position He prepares us for His purpose.

Here are a number of things which God will do in the process of the wait:

God Wants To Beautify Your Life And Make You Whole In the Wait

Isaiah 61:3 gives the assurance that The Spirit of the Lord has been given to us to beautify all the ashy dark things in our lives:

To appoint unto them that mourn in Zion, to give unto them beauty for ashes, the oil of joy for mourning, the garment of praise for the spirit of heaviness; that they might be called trees of righteousness, the planting of the Lord, that he might be glorified. (KJV)

Let us look at it this way. Before, you were living a life that has caused some dark, ugly and broken results. God is using the wait to therefore shed some light on the dark things and beautify the ugly things.

Overall He will do a spiritual beautification, which will make you spiritually whole. To be spiritually whole means that your spirit is free from everything that would cause you to be broken or cause you to have an impure mindset or to involve in impure actions.

God Wants You To Be Single & Whole In The Wait

The problem is that sometimes we go from relationship to relationship because we are afraid of being single. We look at being single as some grave illness.

Some of us only know what it means to depend on our partner for every single thing. When you wait on God He will teach you how to depend on Him. He will cause you to stand strong with no one at your side.

God's plan may include marriage but before this can happen He wants you to love yourself and He will use the single season to show you how to do this. The truth is, you can only truly love a partner when you know how to love your life, and

26

you can only truly know how to love yourself, when you know and love God.

God Wants To Elevate You In The Wait

In addition to helping you develop the right mindset about marriage, God truly wants you to wait now so that you can be elevated from where you are. This elevation will lift you above the hurt of the past and make you a more complete woman or man in God.

My favorite Scripture that really defines the elevating rewards of waiting is Isaiah 40:31.

It says:

But they that wait upon the Lord shall renew their strength; they shall mount up

with wings as eagles; they shall run, and not be weary; and they shall walk, and not faint. (KJV)

This Scripture tells us that when we wait on the Lord, He will renew our strength. So if you are weak in the body, spirit or soul, God will strengthen you in the wait. If you do not know how to stand alone, He will stay with you and show you how to do this.

As you get into the Bible and place your focus on God He will give you renewed strength. This refers to a spiritual renewal. You will no longer be crying after the one who walked away from you or the one from who you walked away. God will turn those tears into joy when you realize God's true plan for your life.

God will use the wait to take you to higher dimensions and after your renewal you will gain massive strength to fly like an eagle. Eagles fly high in the sky; higher than many birds in the world and they are also very wise birds. This is not pride that you will be flying with, but you will possess such a level of confidence and authority that will cause your past hurts to be under you.

Based on the strength that you will get in the wait, you will not get weary nor will you fall, but God will keep you up. The relationship breakup you thought would kill you will not. God will give you the strength as you wait.

Do you want to forfeit this type of strength, elevation or confidence now for an earthly partner? I think not. I can reassure you that this is nothing a man or woman could ever give to you.

In conclusion, **God's Purpose For The Wait** is to take you through a process of:

- Becoming a true worshipper and learning to desire God more than having a partner,
- Getting to know Christ and the importance of developing a relationship with Him,
- Becoming and remaining sexually pure,
- Being healed from past hurts and other spiritual weights,
- Allowing God to cleanse your heart and becoming pure in your emotions,
- Getting to know yourself and God's purpose for your life and
- Understanding the relationship between *the wait* and marriage.

Each of these important aspects of the wait has been addressed in the following chapters.

VICKI L. OLTON

I pray that your life will be transformed!

GOD'S PURPOSE FOR THE WAIT

Chapter Six

GOD USES THE WAIT TO HELP YOU BECOME A WORSHIPPER

But an hour is coming, and is now here, when the true worshipers will worship the Father in spirit and truth. Yes, the Father wants such people to worship Him. [24] God is spirit, and those who worship Him must worship in spirit and truth." (John 4:23-24 - HCSB)

IN THE WAIT GOD WILL TEACH YOU HOW TO BECOME A TRUE WORSHIPPER

We are called to worship God and not man. Sadly some of us have been worshipping and idolizing our partners for years and did not realize. God wants to use the wait now to help you come into alignment with His plan of true worship.

The Meaning of the Word "Worship"

Dictonary.com says that worship is, *"reverent honor and homage to God"*.

In the wait God will transform you into one who continually reverences and respects Him. He is the One who created you and you were created to worship Him.

God Must Be Your No.1 Priority

To be a true worshipper, God and the things of God must now become your no. 1 priority.

If your partner was the no.1 priority, waiting on God changes this. Perhaps you did not know any better because the world teaches us that our husbands, wives etc., are to be first.

Here is what the Bible has to say about putting God first:

Proverbs 16:3 says:

Commit your activities to the Lord, and your plans will be achieved. (HCSB)

Matthew 22:37 also says:

Jesus said unto him, Thou shalt love the Lord thy God with all thy heart, and with all thy soul, and with all thy mind. (KJV)

When you put God first you are agreeing to obey all that He says in His Word. All your thoughts, plans and desires must now be based on what the Word of God says.

There Is Power In Worship

After my breakup I had no one but God. I cried many nights because the emotional pain was heavy, but whenever I worshipped, the weight was lifted as the presence of God came closer and closer to me.

Consider the example of Paul and Silas who prayed and worshipped God in singing. When they did this, it caused the angels to move on their behalf and the prison bars were opened for them:

And at midnight Paul and Silas prayed, and sang praises unto God: and the prisoners heard them.

And suddenly there was a great earthquake, so that the foundations of the prison were shaken: and immediately all the doors were opened, and every one's bands were loosed. (Acts 16:25-16 – KJV)

There are some bonds from the past that God wants to loose from off your life, and it is your worship that will cause this to happen. There is power in worship.

The Lesson Of Worship From The Woman At The Well

When the woman at the well met Jesus, little did she know that she was walking into transformation. Little did she know that she was going to start a life of worship within minutes.

Jesus said to the woman in John 4:23 after much discussion:

But the hour cometh, and now is, when the true worshippers shall worship the Father in spirit and in truth: for the Father seeketh such to worship him. (KJV)

Here Jesus was giving her a complete description of what is expected from the worshipper. He told her that the Father is looking for people who will worship Him **in spirit** and **in truth**.

As you wait with God, just as He taught the woman at the well, God will teach you how to be a true worshipper.

You will not be like those outlined in the Bible who worship only with the lips and not with the heart:

This people draweth nigh unto me with their mouth, and honoureth me with their lips; but their heart is far from me.

But in vain they do worship me, teaching for doctrines the commandments of men. (Matthew 25:8-9 – KJV)

God wants you to worship in the spirit. We cannot do anything for God in the flesh. In other words, we are not worshipping God based on our feelings and for what He does, but we must worship God from a clean heart and spirit. Only then will He accept it as true worship.

The Bible says:

So then they that are in the flesh cannot please God. (Romans 8:8 – KJV)

When the Samaritan woman found out that it was Jesus who was speaking to her, she believed and became excited to tell others about Jesus. Jesus touched her heart and she immediately dropped her pot and speedily ran to evangelize to tell others about Jesus. Fetching water was no longer a priority, but Jesus became her priority.

Worshippers evangelize. Worshippers tell others about Jesus and today God is calling you to be like a woman at the well.

Worship Is A Lifestyle

As mentioned before, we have been originally created to worship God as seen in Revelation 4:11:

Thou art worthy, O Lord, to receive glory and honour and power: for thou hast created all things, and for thy pleasure they are and were created. (KJV)

Here are a few Scriptures, which also speak to the fact that we were created by God to worship Him:

Exodus 20:2-6 says:

I am the LORD thy God, which have brought thee out of the land of Egypt, out of the house of bondage.

Thou shalt have no other gods before me.

Thou shalt not make unto thee any graven image, or any likeness of any thing that is in heaven above, or that is in the earth beneath, or that is in the water under the earth:

Thou shalt not bow down thyself to them, nor serve them: for I the LORD thy God am a jealous God, visiting the iniquity of the fathers upon the children unto the third and fourth generation of them that hate me; (KJV)

Exalt ye the Lord our God, and worship at his footstool; for he is holy. (Psalm 99:5 – KJV)

Exalt the Lord our God, and worship at his holy hill; for the Lord our God is holy. (Psalm 99:9 – KJV)

Wherefore we receiving a kingdom which cannot be moved, let us have grace, whereby we may serve God acceptably with reverence and godly fear:
For our God is a consuming fire. (Hebrews 12: 28-29 – KJV)

Over time I realized that worship was more than signing, but rather a lifestyle that God wanted me to adopt.

We develop a life of worship unto God by reading His Word and living according to the truth of the Bible. The wait is therefore God's call for you to read the Bible more often and live by His outlined commands.

Acts of Worship In The Bible

Here are some powerful acts of worship that we should mimic:

- Paul and Silas singing unto God in prison (Acts 16:24-26).
- The woman who broke the alabaster box and anointed Jesus with the precious oil (Luke 7:36-50).
- The widow giving her last little bit of money to the Lord (Mark 12:41-44) – Again worship here is seen as a sacrifice as we give to the work of God.
- Abraham's obedience to respond to God's command to sacrifice His son

(Genesis 22:12-14) – Simple obedience to God is worship unto Him.

- Jesus surrendering to God's will (Luke 22:41-43) – Availing every part of our body, spirit and soul to God is an act of worship.

GOD'S PURPOSE FOR THE WAIT

Chapter Seven

GOD WANTS TO BECOME YOUR BEST FRIEND IN THE WAIT

You are My friends if you do what I command you. I do not call you slaves anymore, because a slave doesn't know what his master is doing. I have called you friends, because I have made known to you everything I have heard from My Father.
(John 15:14-15 – HCSB)

IN THE WAIT, GOD WILL TEACH YOU HOW TO BECOME HIS BEST FRIEND THROUGH RELATIONSHIP BUILDING

As you wait with God the one thing that He wants to do is develop a friendship with you. He wants to become your best friend.

We Are The Bride of Christ and He is Our Bridegroom

Who do you get up in the morning and talk to first thing? Is it your social media friends, your partner, your parents, your work colleagues, or is it God?

The Psalmist David sacrificed much time for God and sought Him early in the morning.

48

Psalm 63:1 says this:

O God, thou art my God; <u>early will I seek thee</u>: my soul thirsteth for thee, my flesh longeth for thee in a dry and thirsty land, where no water is; (KJV)

David was so connected to God that He made sure God was the focus of the start of his day. Some of us reach for the phone to message our BAE (before anyone else) or to respond to another email from the boss.

If you are not talking to God first thing in the morning, this is the time to reposition God so that you can build a solid relationship with Him and become like His best friend.

We usually do all that it takes to please our partner, but now as you wait God wants to show you the importance of pleasing Him.

Abraham was the one person in the Bible who was called God's friend. His mere obedience and faith granted Him this position.

And the scripture was fulfilled which saith, Abraham believed God, and it was imputed unto him for righteousness: and he was called the Friend of God. (James 2:23 – KJV)

As you wait, God wants to teach you how to be obedient to Him so that your future can be brighter than you past has ever been. He did it for me and He wants to do the same for you.

Chapter Eight

GOD HAS CREATED THE WAIT FOR SEXUAL PURITY

For this is God's will, your sanctification: that you abstain from sexual immorality, so that each of you knows how to control his own body, in sanctification and honor, not with lustful desires, like the Gentiles who don't know God. (1 Thessalonians 4:3-5 – HCSB)

GOD'S PURPOSE FOR THE WAIT

IN THE WAIT GOD WILL HELP YOU BECOME AND REMAIN SEXUALLY PURE

God calls us to live a sexually pure life. Countless hours I spent praying and fasting, and asking God to help me remain pure and He responded. He gave me the grace to maintain sexual purity and to this day I have remained pure.

Keeping The Body Sexually Pure

In this season of waiting God wants you to understand that not only fornication is sin, but other acts such as petting, feeling, penetration by use of the fingers and other objects, and the like are also sources of sexual immorality/impurity.

Let us look at the meaning of the word "fornication".

Fornication means sexual activity outside of marriage.

1 Corinthians 6:18-20 says:

Flee fornication. Every sin that a man doeth is without the body; but he that committeth fornication sinneth against his own body.
What? know ye not that your body is the temple of the Holy Ghost which is in you, which ye have of God, and ye are not your own?
For ye are bought with a price: therefore glorify God in your body, and in your spirit, which are God's. (KJV)

The HCSB version puts it this way:

Run from sexual immorality! "Every sin a person can commit is outside the body. On the contrary, the person who is sexually immoral sins against his own body. Don't you know that your body is a sanctuary of the Holy Spirit who is in you, whom you have from God? You are not your own, for you were bought at a price. Therefore glorify God in your body.

1 Thessalonians 4:3-4 says:

For this is the will of God, even your sanctification, that ye should abstain from fornication:
That every one of you should know how to possess his vessel in sanctification and honour; (KJV)

When we commit fornication we sin against our bodies. This introduces sexual impurity into our lives.

You may ask, "how can sex be impure when God made sex?"

Sex is not impure but the act of disobeying God's commands introduces impurity into our lives. The purpose of sex for quick pleasure with no strings attached or for convenience is impure. The use of sex to determine if someone has what it takes to satisfy you in bed and become your spouse are things that make the act impure. Any alteration or perversion of the pure intention for sex is impure.

You may be saying, "I am going to marry this woman or this man, so nothing is wrong with having sex before we get married. We have already decided to spend the rest of our lives together."

I surely said this and at the end of the day I was totally wrong and sinning against God. Fornication is fornication!

God Uses The Wait To Cleanse You From Ungodly Soul Ties Which Occurred During Sex

God wants us to remain pure because there is a deep spiritual and soul bonding, which takes place during the act of sex. And the truth is, we could have bonded with a whole lot of mess.

The Bible tells us that when a man and woman come together in marriage, they become one:

For this reason a man will leave his father and mother and be joined to his wife, and the two will become one flesh. (Ephesians 5:31 – HCSB)

This oneness happens through the act of sex. Since we are spirit beings spirits can pass from body to body. And the souls become intertwined, creating something called soul ties. Fluids are also transferred in the act of sex.

Imagine having had sex with one person. How many spirits and pieces of different souls are you walking around with, taking into consideration the fact that the person also may have had other partners before you?

The Word of God says:

Flee fornication. Every sin that a man doeth is without the body; but he that committeth fornication sinneth against his own body.

What? know ye not that your body is the temple of the Holy Ghost which is in you, which ye have of God, and ye are not your own?
For ye are bought with a price: therefore glorify God in your body, and in your spirit, which are God's. (1 Corinthians 6:18-20)

How many persons have you had sex with? How many persons have you become one with?

Call them by name and rebuke every body, spirit and soul connection to those persons. Ask God to wash your entire being with the blood of Jesus.

Ungodly Soul Ties Can Even Take Place In Marriage, So WAIT

Though marriage is good, ungodly soul ties can also be formed in a marriage that has not been ordained by God or that happens before God's perfect timing.

Remember as you wait, God is cleaning you inside out and He is also cleaning the other person who is being set apart for you. Marrying the wrong person or marrying before God's timing can cause you to become one with someone at a time when

God has not completed his spiritual cleansing process.

This is why it is vital to ensure that you enter a marriage with the spirit of Jesus on the inside of you and no other spirit or residue from sexual encounters with someone else.

Both individuals must have taken the time to wait and allow God to clean them and prepare them for a marriage in Him.

The Mind Must Also Be Sexually Pure

Remaining sexually pure in the mind is important because according to the Bible, fornication can also take place in the mind/heart beginning with the mere eyes:

Ye have heard that it was said by them of old time, Thou shalt not commit adultery:

But I say unto you, That whosoever looketh on a woman to lust after her hath committed adultery with her already in his heart. (Matthew 5:27-28 – KJV)

This is why it is important to make sure that your thoughts remain clean when you look at someone. If you do not do this, then you can commit fornication in your heart. God is willing to help you remain pure in the mind as He takes you through the wait.

GOD'S PURPOSE FOR THE WAIT

Chapter Nine

IN THE WAIT GOD WILL DESTROY THE ROTTEN ROOTS

But he answered and said, Every plant, which my heavenly Father hath not planted, shall be rooted up. (Matthew 15:13)

GOD WILL USE THE WAIT TO REMOVE SOME DEEP ROOTS THAT HAVE HINDERED YOUR LIFE

God Will Cut Down The Roots Of Hurt And All Related Branches In The Wait

Pain can only be dismissed for so long. It will resurface and hinder every relationship going forward, once it is not dealt with.

Hurting people, hurt others. They carry around weights and burdens that if not dealt with, will show in their behaviors and hinder every area of their lives.

Some of you reading now have experienced a significant amount of emotional, spiritual, physical and mental abuse at the hands of a partner. Now the only thing you have to show from the relationship is low self-esteem, low self worth and shame.

All is not lost. You can have your joy back. You can feel beautiful again but your beauty is not in the validation of man or a woman, it is in the declarations that Jesus has made about you in the Word of God.

The Psalmist talks about His worth in Psalm 139 and we too can apply this to our lives:

For thou hast possessed my reins: thou hast covered me in my mother's womb.

I will praise thee; for I am fearfully and wonderfully made: marvellous are thy works; and that my soul knoweth right well.

My substance was not hid from thee, when I was made in secret, and curiously wrought in the lowest parts of the earth.

Thine eyes did see my substance, yet being unperfect; and in thy book all my members were written, which in continuance were fashioned, when as yet there was none of them. (Psalm 139:13-16 – KJV)

He goes on in verse 17 to confirm that God's thoughts towards us are precious. Man's thoughts may not be precious towards us, but God's surely are:

How precious also are thy thoughts unto me, O God! how great is the sum of them! (Psalm 17 –KJV)

God's thoughts towards us remain pure. This is shown through the writings of John:

Dear friend, I pray that you may prosper in every way and be in good health physically just as you are spiritually (3 John 1:2 – HCSB)

It is Christ's love that must compel us and not the love of man:

For Christ's love compels us, since we have reached this conclusion: If One died for all, then all died. [15] And He died for all so that those who live should no longer live for themselves, but for the One who died for them and was raised. (2 Corinthians 5:14 – HCSB)

God Wants To Cut Down The Roots of Shame In The Wait

There are some things that have been spoken about us and some things that we have done, which have caused the spirit of shame to enter our lives.

With the spirit of shame we will not be courageous enough to answer the call of God for our lives. Similarly, with the spirit of shame we are unable to be confident in relationships and love the way that we should. God will use the wait to remove all shame from our lives so that we can love Him first and then in turn love others and ourselves.

Remember now that you are in Christ:

There is therefore now no condemnation to them which are in Christ Jesus, who walk not after the flesh, but after the Spirit. (Romans 8:1 – KJV)

God Will Help You Cut Down The Roots of Childhood Hurts In The Wait

In the midst of this restart you will realize that a lot of the brokenness that you have experienced has root in experiences from your younger years.

In my season of waiting God began to show me all the rotten roots that were planted in my life from a very young age. Roots such as low self-esteem, low self worth and the need for attention existed and these led me into a life of fornication.

Does this sound familiar?

The great thing is that whatever God has not put in our life, He will root up and destroy.

Scripture tells us:

But he answered and said, Every plant, which my heavenly Father hath not planted, shall be rooted up. (Matthew 15:13)

Some of you have even been raped and that is why you have been caught in the cycle of fornication from very young. You feel worthless, but God loves you and sees you as worth it all. All He wants to do is heal you of the pain and shame so that you can be whole for Him.

Let us therefore come boldly unto the throne of grace, that we may obtain mercy, and find grace to help in time of need. (Hebrews 4:16 – KJV)

There are some things that even your parents and people in authority have spoken over you and have caused your life to go in a direction opposite to what God had originally planned for you. Can you identify?

These roots have also caused you to have a negative view of yourself. God will use His waiting process to remove these things from your life.

God wants to pull up these roots of rejection. He taught me that if I had not dealt with these things, I would not be effective in my Christian walk and most definitely not in a marriage.

The Wait Is The Generational Curse Cleanup Season

Thou shalt not bow down thyself to them, nor serve them: for I the Lord thy God am a jealous God, visiting the iniquity of the fathers upon the children unto the third and fourth generation of them that hate me; (Exodus 20:5 – KJV)

There are also some generational curses and situations, which exist because of the evil done by your ancestors. These roots have caused you to make some really bad decisions in the past as it relates to relationships. Now is the time not only to repent on behalf of your forefathers, but also to forgive those who introduced the wrong things into your life.

There are also some negative behaviors that remain in your bloodline from generation to generation that are affecting and will continue to affect the way you do things. These roots need to be dealt with and cut off so that you can be effective in the Kingdom and purpose of God.

Maybe there are some attitudes from your father or mother that still remain in your mannerisms today. They have only caused them harm and have also caused you harm. These things, if taken into another relationship will continue to produce the same negative results.

Some of you have seen a continuous trend of relationship breakup in every member your family. No one seems to be able to have good relationships and now it has been continually happening to you. This is a curse that needs to be broken.

The waiting period is therefore the time assigned by God for you to commission Him to work on your behalf in order to remove the generational issues in your life so that you can be free.

Chapter Ten

IN THE WAIT GOD WILL FIX YOUR HEART

Create in me a clean heart, O God; and renew a right spirit within me. (Psalm 51:10 – KJV)

GOD WILL USE THE WAIT TO CLEANSE YOUR HEART OF ALL UNFORGIVENESS TOWARDS YOUR EX

You must forgive all who have caused the wrong roots to be planted in your life, and also forgive yourself.

Jesus spoke about forgiveness in Matthew 6:14:

For if ye forgive men their trespasses, your heavenly Father will also forgive you: (KJV)

For if you forgive people their wrongdoing, your heavenly Father will forgive you as well. (HCSB)

I had an abortion. I thought that I had overcome all of the negative emotions. But the resentment and unforgiveness were still there. Though I prayed and asked God to remove these negative emotions, they still attacked my heart. I had to decide to forgive myself and the other person in order to overcome.

Unforgiveness is a weight that sits on our shoulders. It hinders our hearts (feelings) and prevents us from loving the way that God wants us to love. As you allow God to help you to forgive He will give you a heart of love.

The Proverbs tells us that things like envy cause rottenness to our bones. Unforgiveness has the very same negative effect.

The Scripture says:

A sound heart is the life of the flesh: but envy the rottenness of the bones. (Proverbs 14:30 - HCSB)

Negative emotions attract evil spirits. These spirits manifest in our physical bodies in the form of sicknesses. I am sure you do not want to be in a situation like this, so, FORGIVE.

Let go of the other person who has caused you pain in the past relationship(s).

God does not want you to get a heart attack. He wants you to also have normal blood pressure. He wants to take the weight off of your heart and body. He wants to close the door which has allowed the enemy to come in and make you mentally, physically and emotionally sick. Now is the time to FORGIVE.

The Word of God says:

Follow peace with all men, and holiness, without which no man shall see the Lord: Looking diligently lest any man fail of the grace of God; lest any root of bitterness springing up trouble you, and thereby many be defiled; (Hebrews 12: 14-15)

The Proverbs tell us that a merry heart is like medicine. God wants us to know the right emotions are like medicine to our bodies, spirits and souls.

Proverbs 17:22 states:

A merry heart doeth good like a medicine: but a broken spirit drieth the bones. (KJV)

A joyful heart is good medicine, but a broken spirit dries up the bones. (HCSB)

One version says a merry heart and the other says a joyful heart. The Hebrew meaning of the word "merry" is gleeful, glad, joyful and rejoicing.

You may ask, "how can I be gleeful and rejoice when He left me for her after so many years of marriage?" or, "how can I be glad when she took off after I gave her everything?"

Let us look at this for what it really is. God allowed him or her to leave because they were not the one in the first place that you should have been with. They left because they are not part of God's plan for your life. Where God wants to take you, that person does not have what it takes to go there with you.

GOD'S PURPOSE FOR THE WAIT

Chapter Eleven

YOU WILL REDISCOVER YOURSELF AS YOU WAIT

He that findeth his life shall lose it: and he that loseth his life for my sake shall find it.
(Matthew 10:39 – KJV)

GOD WILL USE THE WAIT TO HELP YOU DISCOVER THE REAL YOU AND YOUR GOD-GIVEN PURPOSE

Now that you are restarting your life with God, look into the mirror. As you look, God will help you define that person that you see in the mirror. He will reveal the level of greatness that He placed in you before you were in your mother's womb through the Bible and as you pray and worship Him.

God Will Help You Truly Find Yourself In The Wait

Sometimes your discovery may run deeper than the purpose of God. There are some simple things about you that you have neglected over the years. You may have been so busy trying to please your partner that you neglected to enjoy the simple things of life.

I was so caught up with a relationship back then that I did not know what my favorite color was anymore. My whole identity had just slipped by because I wanted to be a wife to someone who God did not want as a husband for me.

As I restarted my life with God, He also revealed some facts about my personality that I had not known before.

If I ask some of you, "who are you?" you may take a while to respond, because for years you spent time catering to the needs of an earthly relationship and have allowed man to define who you are.

Now is the season to rediscover who you really are. I had to do it and if God brought me through, He will bring you through also.

You Will Discover A Social Life In The Wait

Some of us have spent so much time playing the wife without the official ceremony, ring and blessing of God, that we neglected to develop relationships with others and enjoy ourselves.

After the breakup God took me through a process of exploring relationship building with the people around me. I became more involved in wholesome social activities with close Christian friends, which eventually helped me become a more well-rounded and balanced individual.

God Wants To Reveal Your Purpose to You In The Wait

After a breakup God places you in a position to rediscover yourself as you get closer and closer to Him. As previously mentioned, He will tell you about your purpose and your calling. Sometimes we are so caught up with our partners that we forget ourselves and solely become the one catering to the other person's needs.

The Bible tells us:

For I know the thoughts that I think toward you, saith the Lord, thoughts of peace, and not of evil, to give you an expected end. (Jeremiah 29:11)

The Holy Spirit wants to let you know how important you are to Him and His Kingdom. Others may not have seen how important you are. They may not have seen the awesomeness that God created in you, but God wants to tell you about it.

Prayer Unlocks Purpose

In the wait, God wants to teach you about the power communicating with Him through prayer.

Seek the Lord and his strength, seek his face continually. (1 Chronicles 16:11 – KJV)

Talk to God in prayer and ask Him questions about your purpose, He will respond.

And it shall come to pass, that before they call, I will answer; and while they are yet speaking, I will hear. (Isaiah 65:24)

Call unto me, and I will answer thee, and show thee great and mighty things, which thou knowest not. (Jeremiah 33:3)

God encourages us to call on Him. He encourages us to communicate with Him:

Ask, and it shall be given you; seek, and ye shall find; knock, and it shall be opened unto you:
For every one that asketh receiveth; and he that seeketh findeth; and to him that knocketh it shall be opened. (Matthew 7:7-8)

As you communicate with God, God will tell you through His word that you are special. He will also confirm by revelation, dreams and visions, the plans, which He has for you.

Over time as you continue to pursue God, He will also tell you about the spiritual gifts that He has given to you.

1 Corinthians 12: 4-12 tells us about these gifts:

Now there are diversities of gifts, but the same Spirit.

And there are differences of administrations, but the same Lord.

And there are diversities of operations, but it is the same God which worketh all in all.

But the manifestation of the Spirit is given to every man to profit withal.

For to one is given by the Spirit the word of wisdom; to another the word of knowledge by the same Spirit;

To another faith by the same Spirit; to another the gifts of healing by the same Spirit;

To another the working of miracles; to another prophecy; to another discerning of spirits; to another divers kinds of tongues; to another the interpretation of tongues:

But all these worketh that one and the selfsame Spirit, dividing to every man severally as he will.

For as the body is one, and hath many members, and all the members of that one body, being many, are one body: so also is Christ.

You May Rediscover God's Career Choice For You In The Wait

When God begins to show you what plans He has for you, you may begin to realize that the job you once loved so much is not what God has planned for your future.

When I began to walk with God after my breakup, I was able to discover the deep passion inside of me for ministry. I realized then that I was truly made to be an entrepreneur and as a result, He eventually moved me out of a 9am to 5pm job. Now as a business owner there is greater flexibility to spend quality time with God and prepare for ministry.

God Wants You To Go On Dates With Jesus In The Wait

On your journey of self-discovery, there will be seasons where you will need to just leave the house and go for a walk with Jesus or sit by the seaside or in the park and just commune with Him. I like to call these moments "dates with Jesus".

The same time you spent with your ex, you must now spend that time with Jesus and He will reveal some awesome things to you about yourself in that quiet and private place.

You will begin to love everything about yourself and see yourself in a totally different way. As you spend more and more time with God, not only will He reveal to you the awesomeness of your creation, but also He will tell you that you are beautiful, He will tell you how precious you are and your view of yourself will change significantly.

Chapter Twelve

WORSHIP GOD NOT MARRIAGE

I don't say this out of need, for I have learned to be content in whatever circumstances I am. (Philippians 4:11 – HCSB)

MARRIAGE IS IN THE PURPOSE, BUT NOT THE PURPOSE FOR THE WAIT

Marriage is honorable and good in God's sight according to Hebrews 13:4:

Marriage is honourable in all, and the bed undefiled: but whoremongers and adulterers God will judge (KJV)

However, God does not want you to worship the need for a husband. That is why He uses the wait to teach you how to be a worshipper of God. Of course, God wants the next relationship to be an honorable one, so you must learn to honor God first.

There is indeed a special someone connected to your purpose here on this earth, but you will only get to know that person when you wait on God and allow

Him to mold you into who He wants you to be for Him. Marriage is in the purpose, but marriage is not the main purpose for the wait.

God taught me in the wait that I must never place my focus on being married. When you do this it is likely that you may find yourself more concerned about being married than having a relationship with God.

Such an attitude opens the door for the enemy to bring many counterfeits our way to hinder our walk with God. The wrong focus could also hinder God's process of allowing the divine connection with the one who He has molded for us.

How can you be an effective wife or husband without knowing who you are in God first?

Scriptures say that the husband must love His wife the way that Christ loves the church (adapted from Ephesians 5:25).

How can anyone love their spouse like Christ loved the church when they are not focused on Christ and getting to know Him but rather focused on being married?

The Kingdom of God Must Come First

You must trust God on His Word, let go and let God and whatever God has for you, without a doubt, you can trust that you will get it when the time is right.

All God wants you to do is seek Him and His righteousness so that you can have His nature and do His will. At the allotted time you will get what is for you.

But seek ye first the kingdom of God, and his righteousness; and all these things shall be added unto you. (Matthew 6:33 – KJV)

Jesus was talking about things such as clothing, food, and drink etc. and I add to the list; jobs, husbands and wives. These are the things which God says are ours. When we reposition our hearts on Jesus Christ our lives become easier and He supplies all that we need.

We do not want to end up getting married before the time or when we do get married, we do not want to be unprepared and end up hampering the purpose of God.

God wants a marriage for you where both parties will walk together, not in themselves nor in their own wills, but in Christ, with the same common goal towards honoring God and doing His perfect will.

Remember the Scripture, which says:

Can two walk together, except they be agreed? (Amos 3:3 – KJV)

Therefore:

Rest in the Lord, and wait patiently for him: fret not thyself because of him who prospereth in his way, because of the man who bringeth wicked devices to pass. (Psalm 37:7 – KJV)

VICKI L. OLTON

GOD'S PURPOSE FOR THE WAIT

SPECIAL PRAYERS FOR SINGLES

PRAYER OF FREEDOM FROM THE WORLD'S STANDARD

Father, I ask You to forgive me for anytime I have said something or done something that subconsciously positioned me as fish bait. Lord I recognize that You have made me to be a precious human being and I humbly repent. I apologize for every thought, word and deed that has been done against Your perfect will for my life.

I recognize that when I embrace the standard of the world, it gives the enemy the authority to come into my life and do what he wants. Today I close every single door of the past that has been opened to cause immorality to come into my life, in the name of Jesus.

I declare that my life is covered in the blood of Jesus. I confess that God's standard is what has been given to me to by which I must live.

I pray that You would give me the strength and tenacity to continue to seek after Your standard through reading the Word of God, and walking after Your laws and precepts. Father I thank You for answering my prayer, in Jesus' Mighty Name. AMEN!

PRAYER OF TOTAL SURRENDER

Acts 17:28 says: *For in him we live, and move, and have our being; as certain also of your own poets have said, For we are also his offspring.*

Father, in the name of Jesus I thank You for Your Word and the fact that You are the One who created me and gave me life. Based on this, I have all right to serve You and live for You. Based on this I have all right to worship You.

Today I surrender my entire life to You. I surrender my past, my present and my future to You. I surrender my body, spirit and soul to You Father. May this be the beginning of an entire life change for me. May this be the start of a totally new life of worship.

I surrender my entire will to You. I repent for all the times when I have made decisions based on my own will. I repent for all the times I have pursued a relationship before pursuing You.

I now turn my entire life over to You so that You can prepare me not only for marriage, if it is Your will for my life, but most importantly, prepare me to execute Your purpose here on earth.

Thank You for the change of life. All the desires to make my own decisions and have my own way are rebellion unto You. Forgive me. All this I ask in the Mighty Name of Jesus. AMEN!

PRAYER OF FREEDOM FROM THE RESIDUE OF PAST SINS

Father, I thank You for the freedom which exists in You and You alone. I pray that by the power of the blood of Jesus that You would wipe my body, spirit and soul clean today. All residue that still remains of past sin, I ask that You remove it in the name of Jesus.

I commit my life into Your hands and all the attitudes which have taken preeminence in my life because of sin in the past. I ask that today they be wiped away by Your blood. The residue of deceit, unforgiveness, oppression, resentment and depression that may still exist in my life, today I declare that by Your fire, they are being removed so that I can be all that You have called me to be.

All residues of insecurities and shame, which exists because of past sin, I roast it in the fire of God in the name of Jesus. All insecurities that came about because of the opinion of other partners, I declare today will be no more, because Jesus is the King of my life and in Him is my identity.

All the residue of hurts and other emotions that I have not let go, today I declare the fire of God will locate them and roast them. Wash me in the blood of Jesus. All hidden emotions are exposed today in the name of Jesus. AMEN!

PRAYER FOR SEXUAL PURITY

Father in Your Word You have commanded all to remain sexually pure because our bodies are the temple of Jesus Christ. I pray in the name of Jesus that You would cleanse me of all the past spiritual, emotional and physical transfers which took place in past sexual encounters.

I believe in Your word, so I believe that through the blood of Jesus I am being cleansed right now from sexual impurity. Lord grant me the grace to hold my body from fornication. May You grant me the grace to abstain from any type of activity that would cause me to defile my body and disobey Your commands. I now commit all of my sexual organs to You Father.

I cancel every assignment of every monitoring spirit on my life. The spirits that the enemy has assigned to my life from birth to cause me to fall into fornication, today I roast them in the fire of God, in the name of Jesus.

I cut myself free from every generational curse of fornication. I declare that my generations to come will not operate by this spirit, in the name of Jesus.

Purify me today by Your spirit. Fill me with Your Holy Spirit. Fill me with Your fruit. I declare that the desire for the things of the flesh will not be exalted above the things of Jesus Christ.

I declare that I have the strength to overcome all manner of evil, because according to John 4:4, I have overcome all evil because greater is He that is in me than he who is in the world.

I take the authority based on the power that You have given to me to trample on serpents, scorpions and over all power of evil.

Father I pray for a cleansing of the mind so that my thoughts remain sexually pure. I rebuke every spirit of lust and perversion that would seek to urge me to commit adultery or fornication in my heart. All this, I ask in the Mighty Name of Jesus. Amen!

PRAYER TO DESTROY THE POWER OF UNGODLY SOUL TIES

Father in the name of Jesus I break every ungodly soul tie. I cancel every connection created from past sexual and other relationships. I call down the fire of God on every spiritual, emotional and physical transfer, which took place, in the name of Jesus. Father cleanse me by the power of the blood of Jesus, in the Mighty Name of Jesus.

Every attitude and alterations that took place in my life based on spiritual transfers I pray today in the name of Jesus that by Your power, You would cleanse me and set me free.

I speak a cleansing by the blood of Jesus into my DNA and I declare destruction to every alteration of my DNA caused by the passing of bodily fluids during sexual activity. May my entire life be made pure through the blood of Jesus. I declare that Your print is written on my DNA, in the name of Jesus.

Every ungodly soul tie that was created in my life as a result of ungodly friendships, I pray today that these ungodly ties would be severed by the sword of the Holy Ghost in the name of Jesus.

Today I declare that my soul is tied to You, my Heavenly Father in the name of Jesus. I tie my body, my soul and my spirit to You in the Mighty Name of Jesus. AMEN!

GOD'S PURPOSE FOR THE WAIT

Acknowledgements

All Praises be to God!!!

First of all I acknowledge the King of Kings and Lord of Lords.

Special gratitude goes continually to my pastor Apostle Marguerite Breedy-Haynes; a great mentor in my life. May God continue to bless her as she continues the work of saving the lost at any cost in these end times.

Gratitude is also extended to all those who were and continue to be instrumental in my waiting process as God continues to beautify me for His special purpose.

BIBLIOGRAPHY

1. Strong, James. Strong's Expanded Exhaustive Concordance of the Bible. Nashville: Thomas Nelson, 2009.

2. Wait. In Dictionary.com. Retrieved from http://www.dictionary.com/browse/wait?s =t

3. Worship. In Dictionary.com. Retrieved from http://www.dictionary.com/browse/worshi p?s=t

Thank You for Reading!

If you enjoyed this book and found it useful, I would be very grateful if you would post a short review on Amazon.

Your support really does make a difference and I read all the reviews personally so I can get your feedback and make this and other books even better.

Should you have any questions, prayer requests, or would like to share a testimony, you can email me at contact@vickiolton.com.

ABOUT THE AUTHOR

Vicki L. Olton is a Christian author and speaker. She is also the founder & president of Mission Inside Out (Barbados). Through the Mission, Vicki's aim is to help persons find hope through Christ in order to live a more purpose-driven life.

Vicki is dedicated to educating persons on true beauty in Christ and how to live a balanced Christian life. Vicki is also an intercessor, preacher, mentor and global marketing consultant. She is a strong agent of change in the lives of others and continues to be a living testimony of the powerful and precious saving grace of God.

OTHER BOOKS BY VICKI

G☺D'S PERFECT TIMING

EMBRACING GOD'S WILL FOR YOUR LIFE

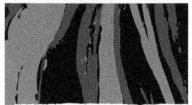

G☺D'S PERFECT TIMING

EMBRACING GOD'S WILL FOR YOUR LIFE

VICKI L. OLTON

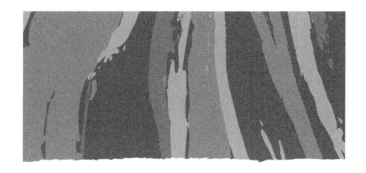

EL TIEMP🕐
PERFECTO DE DIOS

ABRAZANDO LA VOLUNTAD DE DIOS PARA SU VIDA

Enseñanza y Diario de Oración Semanal por:

VICKI L. OLTON

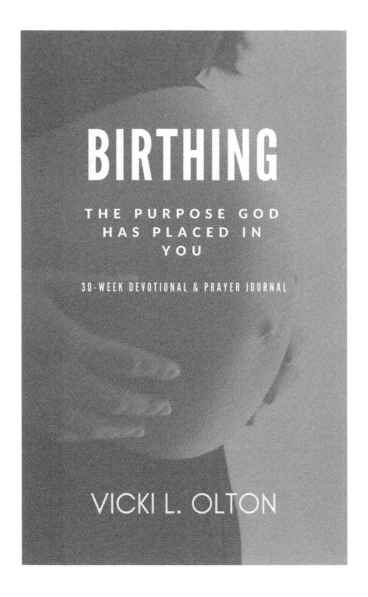

All of Vicki's books can be bought on

Amazon.com

CONTACT DETAILS

PROPHETESS VICKI OLTON

Website: www.vickiolton.com

Facebook: Prophetess Vicki Olton

Instagram: prophetess_vicki_olton

Email: contact@vickiolton.com

MISSION INSIDE OUT

Website: theinsideoutmission.wordpress.com

Facebook: Mission Inside Out

Instagram: Mission Inside Out

Email: theinsideoutmission@gmail.com

GOD'S PURPOSE FOR THE WAIT

JOURNAL

_____

_____

_____

_____

_____

_____

_____

_____

_____

_____

_____

_____

_____

_____

_____

_____

_____

VICKI L. OLTON

_____

_____

_____

_____

_____

_____

_____

_____

_____

_____

_____

_____

_____

_____

_____

_____

_____

_____

_____

_____

_____

_____

_____

_____

_____

_____

_____

_____

_____

_____

_____

_____

_____

_____

_____

_____

_____

_____

_____

_____

_____

_____

GOD'S PURPOSE FOR THE WAIT

_____

_____

_____

_____

_____

_____

_____

_____

_____

_____

_____

_____

_____

_____

_____

_____

_____

_____

_____

_____

_____